Inspirations of the Heart

MICHAEL BERNARD BECKWITH

ARTISTIC EXPRESSIONS
BY F. RASSOULI

AGAPE GLOBAL VENTURES • LOS ANGELES, CALIFORNIA

QUOTATIONS AND AFFIRMATIONS: MICHAEL BERNARD BECKWITH
ARTISTIC EXPRESSIONS: F. RASSOULI

ARTISTIC DIRECTOR: KUWANA HAULSEY
EDITOR (QUOTES): KUWANA HAULSEY
EDITOR (TEXT): ANITA REHKER
COVER AND BOOK DESIGN: TRISH WEBER HALL • WWW.TRISHWEBERSTUDIO.COM

PUBLISHER: AGAPE GLOBAL VENTURES
5700 BUCKINGHAM PARKWAY
CULVER CITY, CA 90230
WWW.AGAPELIVE.COM/INSPIRATIONS

LIBRARY OF CONGRESS CATALOGING-IN-PUBLICATION DATA
ISBN: 0-9700327-2-2

PRINTER: STAR STANDARD PRINTING (SINGAPORE)

--- DEDICATIONS ---

To my grandfather Francis Bernard Beckwith, Sr. (Chief)
– I thank you for teaching me to be a giver.

To my parents Alice G. Beckwith & Francis Bernard Beckwith, Jr.
– I thank you for a strong foundation of love and dreams.

To my children Kiilu Francis Fanon Beckwith & Micaela Ayana Alice Beckwith
– I thank you for choosing me as your parent.

To my wife Rickie Byars Beckwith – I thank you for being in my life
as the music, love and so much more. Thank You.

Michael

To Gitty, who has been my support when I'm down
and my encouragement when I'm up in my life's journey.

Rassouli

We walked into this life as a magical gift to the world, a gift crafted by divine hands and a donation to the mystery of being. As such, we are perfection in the making, artisans of beauty, the voice of the cosmos whispering through every breath the enchanting purity and mystery of life.

Each day constitutes a page of the book of our art that we must read aloud into the heart's ears of our brothers and sisters. We have a duty to contribute to the cosmic encyclopedia pre-designed by the divine. Thus, our calling is to art, the home of our being and the ground of expression of our true power.

Inspirations of the Heart is a rendition of what the landscape of our being looks like and feels like. Its pages are a road map of the artistic unfolding initiated at the time of our birth, which beckons us to bask in the sea of our fullness as a gift to the world. They open their arms in prayer for the honey of living to drip into the secret recesses of our being.

They kindle the fire that expands the psyche wide enough to see the overwhelming truth of our greatness.

These pages ask us to slow down, to reduce our pace of living, and to notice the lofty softness of the duvet that envelops us at all times. Each page is a vortex of beauty uttering the chant of eternal life as art and testifying to our infinite capacity to love. In a world where distraction tends to limit us from this realization and fosters a spirit of smallness, these pages are an invitation to rise into a sense of greatness never before thought of as possible.

Here, we are invited to visit the garden of Spirit and to take a sip of the nectar of the soul, the magic potion that swells the heart into a deeper rhythm with the Infinite and awakens our hidden gifts. Life becomes stale without the scent of each blossoming plant in the garden of our being. It is in this garden that we as plants join in a cosmic symphony of colors and sounds, lulled by the whisper of divine rhythm.

In this magical concert our hearts echo, with each throb, the magnificent cadence of the Infinite.

Inspirations of the Heart challenges us to take a hard look into our fears and to see beyond their minimizing effects the incommensurable brilliance of our being. Let us then all respond to this wave of hope gifted to us by these pages and join in a circle of prayer and celebration of love and life. Breathe in the nectar of each page and notice the availability of infinity at your fingertips. Join in the concert and watch yourself change immensely.

Malidoma Patrice Somé is an internationally renowned teacher and author of the books: *Ritual: Power, Healing and Community, Of Water and The Spirit, The Healing Wisdom of Africa,* and *The Gift of the Gatekeeper.*

Art, the word we use in our everyday language to describe creative expression, is nothing less than heaven's own kiss of inspiration. We love all art forms because they reveal the magic of the soul and link our human creativity with that of Divine Creativity, the expression of the Creator of Life itself.

All that we thrill to in the arts is a manifestation of the ultimate Beauty and Mystery of life. When our creative channel is opened, it allows us to caress the sacred face of the Divine. Thus, the arts uplift us, they bring tears to our eyes, they hush us into silence with their profound imprint.

In our fast-paced society we are frequently—though sometimes unconsciously—conditioned to be consumers rushing here and there to satisfy our human needs. Art becomes the soul's resting place. It acts as a cosmic transport wherein we encounter a soul-soothing release of human concerns and embrace divine perfection.

Above all, art touches the core of our spiritual nature. When we use art as a means of embracing Spirit, we come to understand that our lived-life is our art. Moreover, through combining art and meditation, we are able to access an extraordinarily powerful conduit into the silent heart of our being.

Meditation is one of the most profound techniques for cultivating an awakened consciousness. One form of meditation is contemplative meditation, wherein one takes an inspirational statement into meditative awareness and plumbs the depth of its truth.

Resting meditatively in one's own heart creates an expanded perception and offers a glimpse into the mystery of Reality. Contemplating statements of universal truth is a dynamic introduction to meditation.

So I invite you to this practice by selecting a quote from the book you now hold in your hands. Sit quietly, in a relaxed way. Read your chosen quote silently to yourself, then aloud. Breathe. You may, perhaps, choose to close your eyes. As you feel your mind getting still, gently ask your heart to reveal the deeper meaning embedded within the written words.

Keeping your focus on the breath, allow yourself to be enveloped by the peace that rises naturally from within. Then, in stream of consciousness writing, record in a journal or notebook whatever messages are spoken into the sacred stillness of your being.

As you read this book, may you feel the power of the affirmative truth statements it contains. May your heart soar as your eyes absorb the beauty of its *Fusionart* images by Rassouli. The combination of the art and the written word, when taken into meditative contemplation, serves as an opening to access a greater dimension of oneself and is a source of elevation to that dimension. Every page is a prayer in the universal language of Beauty.

May you pray often.

$\mathcal{Y}$OU ARE

THE *Universe in Miniature,*

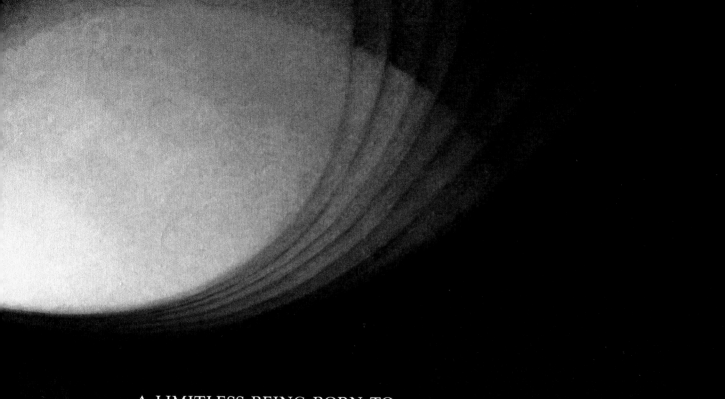

A LIMITLESS BEING BORN TO

REVEAL THE *Hidden Splendor* OF YOUR SOUL.

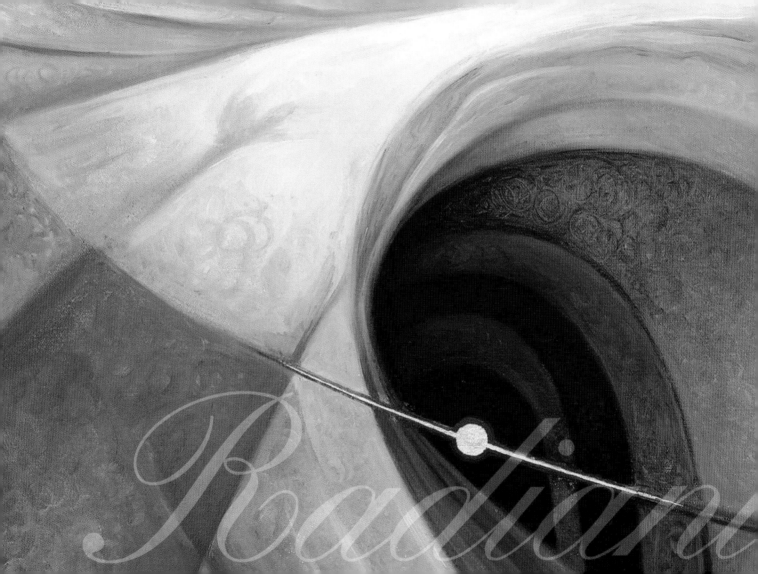

$\mathcal{I}$ AM

A *Radiant* EMANATION OF LIGHT,

A FOUNTAIN OF *Infinite Possibility*

EXISTING TO *Pour* MYSELF INTO EXPRESSION.

I AM

A VESSEL OF THE *Infinite*, FILLED WITH THE
Glorious Peace of God.

Peace

I choose to offer this Peace freely to every man, woman, and child on Earth.

$\mathcal{A}$GLOW

WITH THE LIGHT OF THE DIVINE,

I SURRENDER MY WHOLE ATTENTION

TO THE PRESENCE OF TRUTH

THAT GUIDES MY PATH.

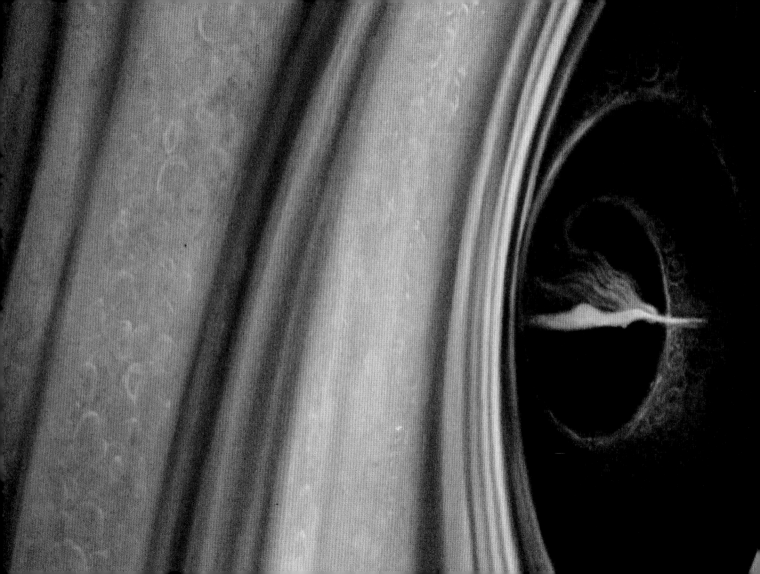

WHEN

YOU SURRENDER TO SPIRIT,

Eternity

BREAKS INTO TIME AS

Your Consciousness,

MANIFESTING ITSELF AS

Your Life.

BE AWARE OF THIS ETERNAL FLOW

AS YOU SOAR FROM GLORY TO

GOD'S GREATER GLORY.

$\mathcal{B}$ELOVED,

STEAL AWAY

MY UNDERSTANDING TONIGHT

AND REPLACE IT WITH *Faith* BY MORNING.

POUR THE NECTAR OF LOVE AND THE HONEY OF

REALIZATION UPON MY TONGUE. LET ME DRINK

UNTIL THEY ARE **One and the Same.**

$\mathcal{M}$IRACLES

ARE SIMPLY INSIGHTS INTO THE

True Nature OF MY BEING.

$\mathcal{A}$CCESS

THE VISION *Within*

AND YOU WILL FIND THAT YOUR MOMENTS OF

High Inspiration

BECOME THE NEXT STAGE

OF YOUR *Evolution.*

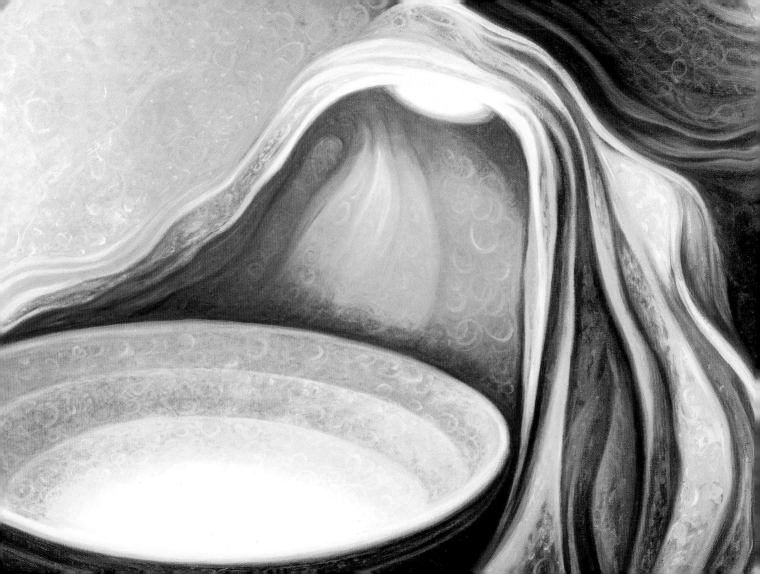

In God

I FIND THE DESIRE BEYOND ALL DESIRING.

In Grace
I find the *Ecstasy of Fulfillment.*

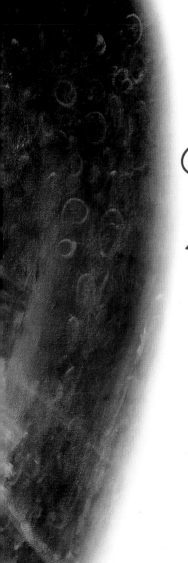

WE STAND

AS A *Midpoint* BETWEEN
Heaven and Earth,

CONSCIOUSLY COMMUNING

WITH THE DIVINE LIGHT OF *Love.*

WE ARE ENFOLDED IN ITS PRESENCE

AND CONSUMED BY ITS AWESOME *Beauty.*

$\mathcal{L}$IFE

IS NOT A PROBLEM TO BE SOLVED,

BUT A **Mystery** TO BE *Lived.*

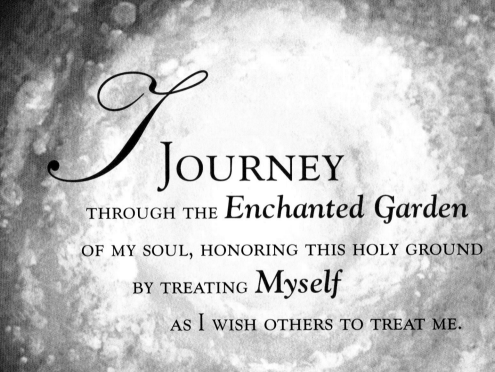

I Journey

THROUGH THE *Enchanted Garden*

OF MY SOUL, HONORING THIS HOLY GROUND

BY TREATING *Myself*

AS I WISH OTHERS TO TREAT ME.

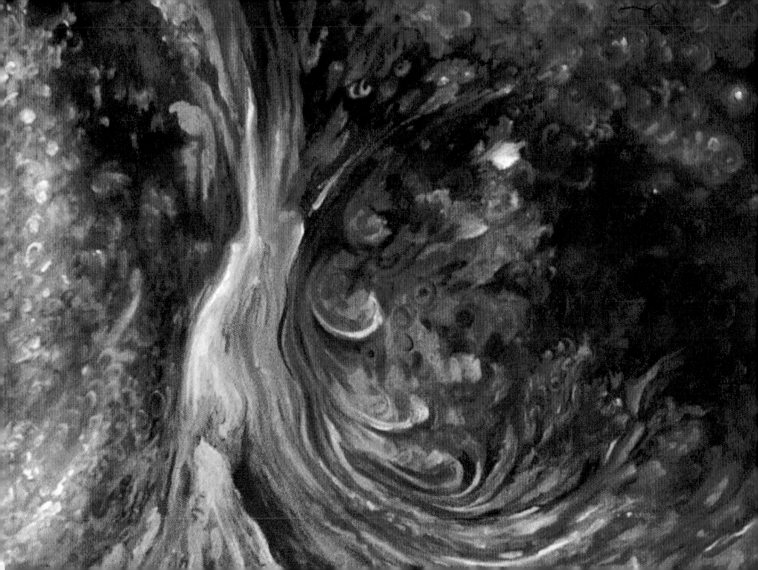

$\mathcal{D}$ISCOVER
the Landscape of Your Soul.

BREAK FREE OF TIME AND ALLOW

THAT WHICH IS ETERNAL

TO *Emerge.*

*I*F YOU ARE NOT LIVING IN *Joy,* YOU ARE OUT OF *Integrity* WITH YOUR *Soul.*

OPEN MINE EYES THAT I MAY SEE ALL
OF *Your Glorious Wonders.*
LET MY ATTENTION BE *Blessed.*
LET MY EYESIGHT BE TURNED TO *Insight*.

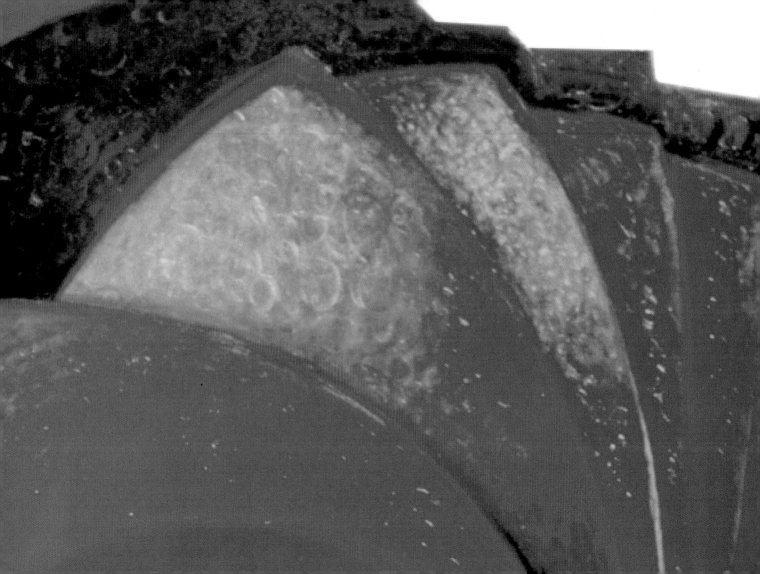

 **A**LL OF LIFE

IS IN *Ecstasy* BECAUSE IT SEEKS NOT TO BE

ANYTHING OTHER THAN WHAT IT IS.

ALLOW THE DIVINE IDEA WITHIN YOU TO UNFOLD.

IT IS YOUR MANDATE.

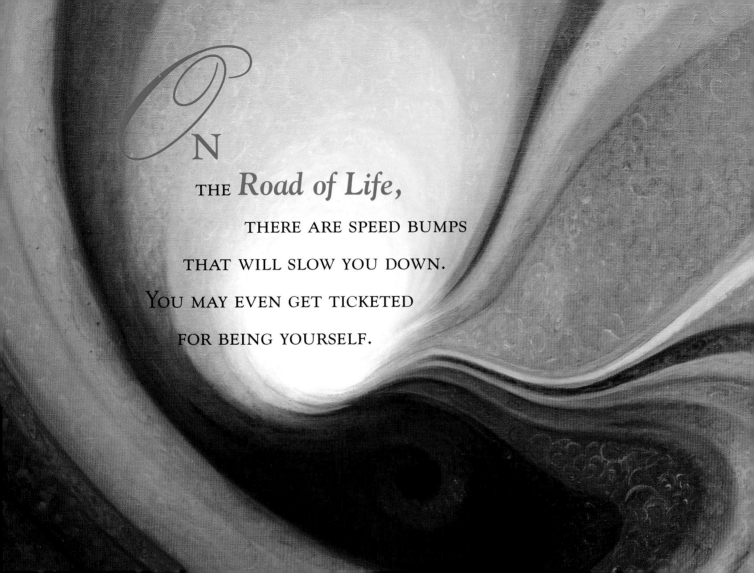

ON

THE *Road of Life,*

THERE ARE SPEED BUMPS

THAT WILL SLOW YOU DOWN.

YOU MAY EVEN GET TICKETED

FOR BEING YOURSELF.

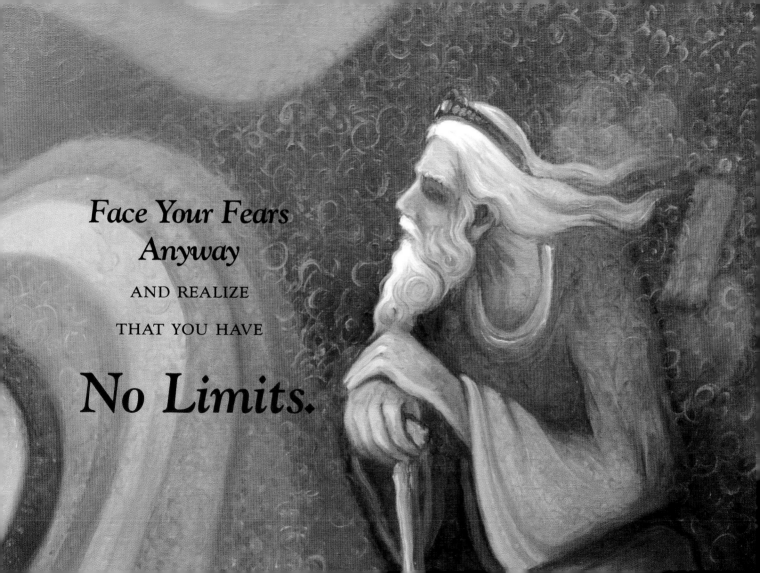

Face Your Fears
Anyway

AND REALIZE

THAT YOU HAVE

No Limits.

THE FLAME

OF GOD IS ALWAYS *Alight*

Within YOU.

THROUGH *Whole-souled* DEVOTION,

YOU UNLEASH ITS *Brilliance*

AND CALL IT FORTH.

votion

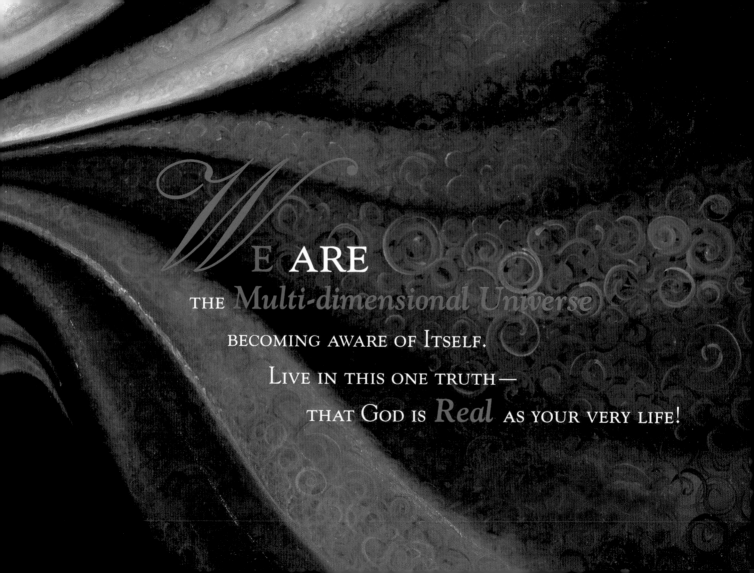

WE ARE THE *Multi-dimensional Universe* BECOMING AWARE OF ITSELF. LIVE IN THIS ONE TRUTH— THAT GOD IS *Real* AS YOUR VERY LIFE!

I AM

THE *Delight* OF GOD,

THE HOLY THOUGHT OF THE *Infinite*

IN LOVING CONTEMPLATION OF ITSELF.

$\mathcal{I}$ AM
A SINGULAR MANIFESTATION
OF A COSMIC
Destiny.

OUR

Hidden Talents and Gifts

THRIVE IN THE LIGHT OF OUR

Pure Intention.

AS WE RELEASE THIS LIFE ENERGY,

THE POWER WITHIN

Blossoms

AS AN EXPRESSION

OF BEING.

$\mathcal{B}$ELOVED,

I long for You in

dark moments, knowing

nothing but

Your Smile

as

Light.

Immerse MYSELF

IN AN EVERLASTING SEA OF CONSCIOUSNESS,

WHERE EVERYTHING IS AVAILABLE AND

All Things Are Possible.

$\mathcal{S}$EEK

TO *Know God*

RATHER THAN USE GOD

TO GET WHAT YOU WANT.

THE POWER BEHIND THIS *Intention*

WILL LIFT YOU BEYOND WORLDLY BOUNDARIES

INTO THE *Transcendent* NATURE

OF YOUR BEING.

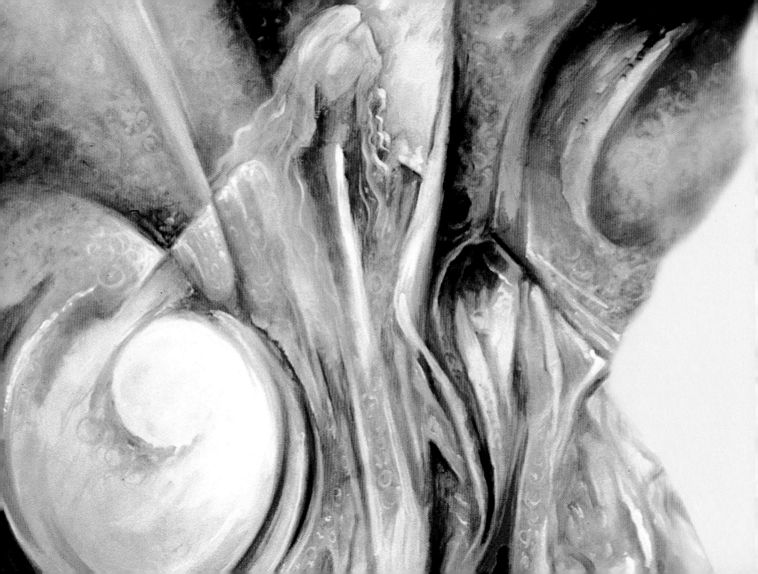

EE

YOURSELF AT THE

Center of the Universe

STANDING BEFORE THE ALTAR OF FAITH

IN THE TEMPLE OF YOUR LIFE.

Listen... THE DIVINE PLAN IS REVEALING ITSELF

AS YOU.

$\mathcal{T}$HERE IS A *Sacred Calling*

WITHIN YOU BEYOND TIME AND SPACE,

FOREVER HOUNDING YOU

TO BE MORE.

YIELD TO IT.

Infinite

To be in league with the infinite
is to be a *Benediction*
wherever you go.

A CELEBRATION

IS GOING ON IN EVERY POINT OF THE UNIVERSE.

GOD IS ANNOUNCING ITSELF AS ME, REJOICING

IN THE *Uniqueness of My Beauty*

AND THE *Oneness* OF MY

SOUL WITH ALL OF LIFE.

WHOLENESS

RESIDES AT THE *Core* OF MY BEING.

MY HEART, MIND, BODY AND SOUL

Drink of the Eternal Waters

FROM WHICH I AM CREATED.

Rejoice!

I Throw Myself Open Wide,
ABANDONING ALL FEAR,
NEGATIVE REACTION
AND LIMITING POINTS OF VIEW.
IN GRATITUDE I REJOICE, KNOWING
THAT SPIRIT RESPONDS BY
CORRESPONDING TO ITS
Divine Nature in Me!

$\mathcal{L}$ISTEN DEEPLY
TO THE *Still, Small Voice* IN YOUR SOUL.
LET IT RAISE YOU ABOVE THE ORBIT
OF CONFUSION AND DOUBT
UNTIL YOU ARE FLYING IN THE SPIRIT
OF THE *Living God.*

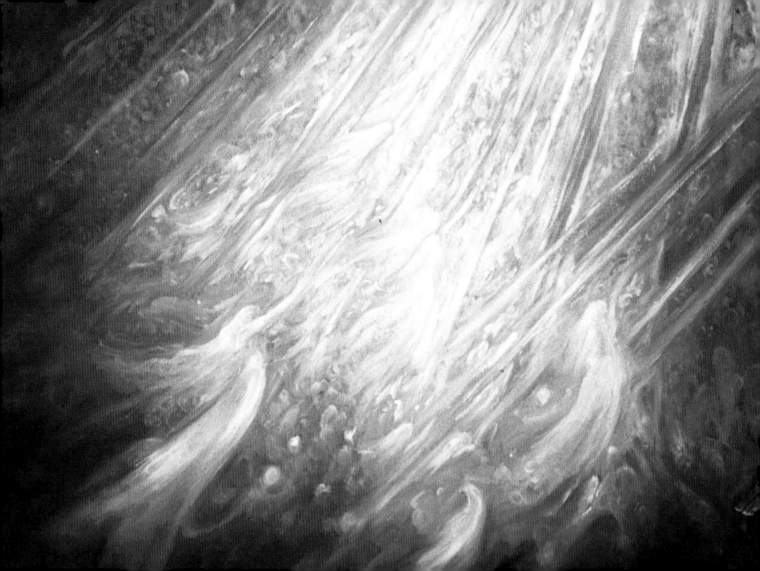

$\mathscr{A}$SK

AND YOU SHALL RECEIVE.

$\mathscr{G}$IVE AND YOU SHALL

Receive Beyond All Asking.

I AM
THE *Music* AND THE INSTRUMENT
OF THE *Most High*!
MY EVERY THOUGHT, WORD
AND ACTION REFLECTS THE LAVISH
BEAUTY OF *Spirit Within.*

THE EDGE

Is An Illusion.

ACKNOWLEDGEMENTS

To my artistic director, Kuwana Haulsey – my heartfelt gratitude for her editing talents,
creativity, spiritual beauty and tireless energy that profoundly contributed to
the birth of this book. She was sent directly from Spirit and I am grateful!

To Anita Rehker, my editor, who added a rich dimension,
as she always does, to this body of work.

To Trish Weber-Hall for her divinely inspired design work which crafted
a dynamic synthesis between the image and the written word.

To Rev. Marcia Anderson for her eye for beauty.

Michael Bernard Beckwith

I would like to thank Dr. Michael Beckwith for his spiritual guidance and openness to
the idea of this book. Also, I would like to thank my daughter, Neda, and Farbod Sadjadi for their
dedicated efforts in putting together the initial design and graphics. I am indebted, as always, to
what I am continuously learning from Rumi, Hafiz and William Blake.

F. Rassouli

With vibrant hues, *Fusionartist* F. Rassouli produces the joyful color blends and circular brushwork that distinguishes his remarkable painting style. Derived from near-eastern spirituality and a foundation in European painting technology, Rassouli's mystical *Fusionart* has garnered worldwide attention in recent years.

Rassouli was born in Isfahan, Iran where he was recognized as the "Best Student Artist in Iran" at age 15 and awarded a government grant to study painting in Europe. He migrated to the United States in 1963, where he studied painting and architecture at the University of New Mexico and USC. While at USC, he was honored with the Leadership Award from the Institute of International Education.

Rassouli's worldwide exhibits include numerous solo and collective shows as well as international art expositions. Over the years he has created hundreds of artworks that have been featured in many books and publications.

To view the full image of the paintings detailed in this book please visit Rassouli's website:

WWW.RASSOULI.COM

LIST OF PLATES IN ORDER OF APPEARANCE

Cover: **WINEGIVER'S ARRIVAL**, 1996 40" x 50"

Foreword: **DISTANT FIFER**, 2000 30" x 40"

TWO INFINITIES, 1995 48" x 60"

BEYOND THE RAINBOW, 2000 24" x 30"

THE OFFERING, 2003 36" x 48"

MYSTIC TRAVELER, 2000 30" x 30"

INFINITE JOURNEY, 1998 36" x 48"

PRAYER FOR THE EARTH, 2001 30" x 40"

EXALTATION, 1995 48" x 60"

THE GIFT, 1998 40" x 40"

THE PEARL, 1999 30" x 30"

ASCENT TO LOVE, 2004 30" x 48"

EVER EXPANDING REALITY, 1995 50" x 65"

ENCHANTED GARDEN, 2001 36" x 48"

THE ULTIMATE FLIGHT, 1998 36" x 48"

PILGRAM OF PASSION, 2003 36" x 36"

THE VISION, 1993 54" x 54"

THE UNFOLDING, 1996 36" x 36"

THE WAYFARER, 1996 54" x 54"

THE DANCE, 1998 36" x 48"

THE VOYAGER, 1995 48" x 60"

A MOMENT IN ETERNITY, 2003 30" x 40"

TWILIGHT OF PERCEPTION, 2000 30" x 40"

BLOOMING, 2000 24" x 30"

LURE OF THE WINEGIVER, 1995 30" x 40"

BRINGER OF THE DAWN, 2000 48" x 60"

LIGHT DANCE, 2001 48" x 60"

ONE SOUL, 2002 30" x 40"

THE SUMMONS, 2002 33" x 48"

VEILING OF THE SOUL, 2004 48" x 72"

THE DROP AND THE OCEAN, 2002 36" x 48"

JOY OF FREEDOM, 2000 30" x 40"

KINDRED SPIRIT, 2001 48" x 72"

SHOWER OF NECTAR, 2001 32" x 32"

THEOPHANIC LIGHT, 1998 30" x 40"

CELESTIAL SONG, 2002 22" x 44"